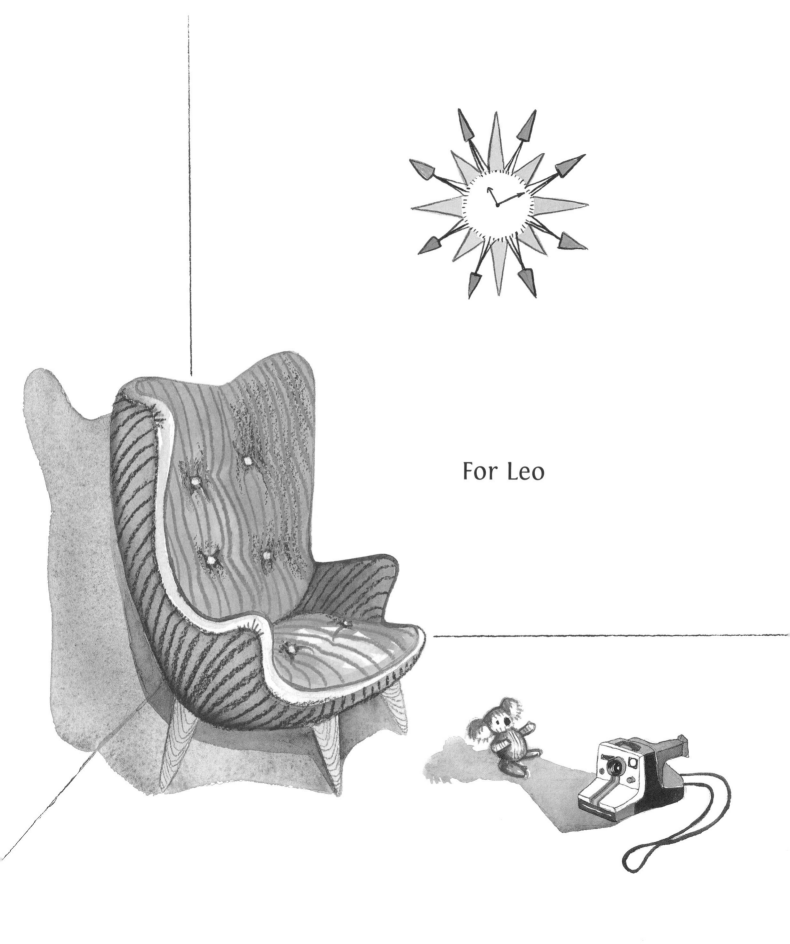

For Leo

The Family Hour

in Australia

by TAI SNAITH

Thames & Hudson

As the sun comes up, the colourful Gouldian finch family eats their breakfast. Mum and Dad finch catch insects and feed their babies together. Good morning finches!

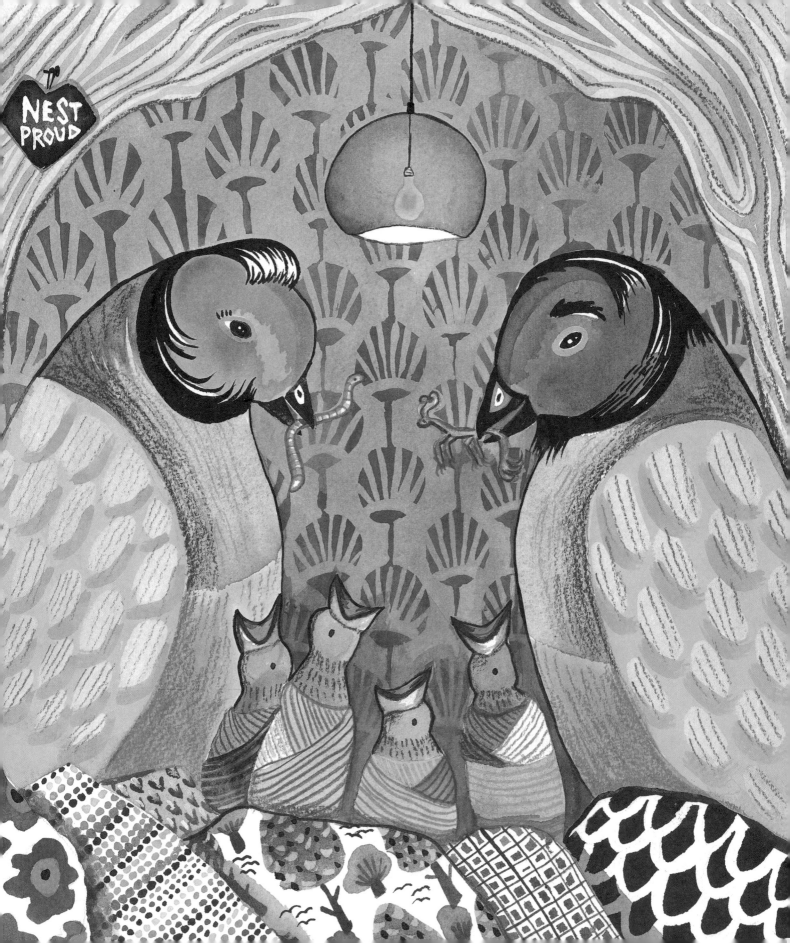

How about some termites for morning tea?
When baby numbats are born they drink milk
from their mum. When they are six months old,
they eat termites by scooping them up with their
long sticky tongues. Crunch, crunch, yum ...

A kangaroo mum can have babies of three different ages at the same time! Can you believe it? A tiny one in her tummy waiting to be born, a small one in her pouch, and a bigger one outside her pouch, called a joey.

Feeling hungry,
the platypus family
goes swimming to
search for snacks.
Did you know they
swim with their
eyes closed?
They use their bills
to search in the mud
and sand for food.

The clever echidna mum feeds her baby
pink milk until it is ready to eat ants.
This cute slurping baby is called a puggle.

Sometimes, two big black swan dads sit on eggs and raise baby swans together. The babies are called cygnets. With two strong dads to protect them, the cygnets have a better chance of surviving.

The glamorous frill-necked lizard mum lays up to ten eggs. The weather affects how many sons and daughters she has. In very hot or very cold weather, more daughters hatch out. How spectacular!

The snoozy koala family spends much of
the day sleeping up high in shady gum trees.
Shhhhhh, it's quiet time for koalas.

In the weedy seadragon family, the hard-working dad carries the eggs. Soon, hundreds of babies hatch out. The dad looks after them until they are big enough to start life alone.

Sugar gliders like to share. Sometimes as many as six or seven mums and dads live together in one nest with all their babies. At dinner time they share a meal. They find sweet things especially delicious.

The eastern spotted quoll family spends each day in one of their many homes. Some homes are in burrows and some are among rocks. Sometimes you might even find them living in farm sheds with the tractors and tools.

The ringtail possum family sleeps all day in their nest, which is called a drey. At night they wake up and feed on leaves, fruit and flowers. Wouldn't it be fun to stay up late?

Tasmanian devils love playing late at night. They wrestle, bite and make lots of terrible noises, like grrrrr and rowwwwl and yellllp!

A corroboree frog dad sings
lovely songs as he minds
his eggs day and night.
He builds his stylish nest
beside a pond so that when
his eggs hatch into tadpoles,
they can swim away.

The cuddly hairy-nosed wombat family shares a burrow. At night they eat and play. As the sun rises they go to sleep. Good night, wombats. Or perhaps that should be good morning!

FAMILY FACTS

GOULDIAN FINCHES **EN**

Gouldian finch mums lay four to eight eggs in a tree hollow. When they hatch, the baby birds are fed insects. Usually finches eat grass seeds, but insects have more protein. Protein helps baby birds grow big and strong. Sometimes several families share one tree hollow.

NUMBATS **EN**

Numbat mums have no pouch. The babies must cling to their mum's hair. They leave their mum when they are one year old. By then they are ready to have babies themselves. Numbats live in hollow logs.

KANGAROOS

A newborn kangaroo weighs only as much as a paperclip or button. The tiny pink baby climbs into its mum's pouch. It clings to a teat that isn't being used by an older joey. Kangaroo mums make one type of milk for the tiny joey, and a different type for the older joey. In bad droughts, unborn joeys stop growing until times are better.

PLATYPUSES

A platypus doesn't use its eyes, ears or nostrils when it hunts underwater. Its sensitive bill detects food. Prey emit weak electrical charges, which the platypus can sense with its bill. It can also feel prey as it searches in the mud and sand.

ECHIDNAS

Echidna milk is pink because it contains iron. Iron also gives blood its red colour. Baby echidnas hatch out of eggs. They grow in their mum's pouch until their spines become too prickly. An echidna's spines protect it from danger.

BLACK SWANS

Black swans usually pair for life. Sometimes two males pair; sometimes two females pair. Often a male and a female pair. Sometimes a male pair of swans collect unwanted eggs. One male may mate with a female. After she lays eggs he pushes her away. Then both male swans care for the eggs and cygnets.

FRILL-NECKED LIZARDS

Frill-necked lizards lay soft-shelled eggs in a nest. Then they bury them. After that, they don't care for the eggs. The young hatch after two months or so. The baby frill-necks stay together for a week or more.

KOALAS

Koalas are the only animals without a tail that live in trees. They eat eucalyptus leaves, which make most other animals sick. The baby drinks milk until it is a year old. When it is old enough to eat leaves, the koala mum feeds it pap from her body. The pap helps the baby digest the leaves.

WEEDY SEADRAGONS **NT**

The seadragon dad is unusual. Most animal dads don't care for their babies. Some that do are seahorses, pipefish, catfish, some frogs and a giant water bug. These dads all take care of their eggs like the seadragon does.

EASTERN SPOTTED QUOLLS **NT**

Quoll mums have six nipples, so only six babies can survive. When the babies are too big for her pouch, she puts them in a den. She carries them on her back when she moves to a new den. Sometimes females share a den with a male. But males don't share with other males.

SUGAR GLIDERS

Sugar gliders spend most of their lives in trees. They glide through the forest in search of sweet gum, nectar and insects. The strongest male uses his scent to mark territory. He also marks the members of his clan. Sugar gliders fight off other gliders that don't belong to their clan.

RINGTAIL POSSUMS

Ringtail possums build a round nest or drey out of grass and bark. It is as big as a football. Ringtails spend most of their time in trees and very little time on the ground. Ringtail fathers are the only possums that help care for their young.

TASMANIAN DEVILS **EN**

Tasmanian devils look and sound fierce. They scream and growl to frighten other devils away from their food. Mostly they eat animals that are already dead. They crunch up even big bones and skulls and swallow fur and feathers. This helps keep the bush clean.

CORROBOREE FROGS **CR**

Sometimes a corroboree frog dad attracts several frog mums to his nest. They lay eggs in the nest. He minds the eggs throughout summer until they are ready to hatch. When rains flood the nest, the tadpoles hatch. They swim into the nearby pool. Their dad has already left by then.

HAIRY-NOSED WOMBATS

Hairy-nosed wombats live in hot dry country without water. They get fluid from eating juicy grasses and shoots. A baby wombat stays in its mum's pouch for six to nine months. It still drinks milk until it is about a year old.

NEAR THREATENED ENDANGERED CRITICALLY ENDANGERED

This book is written and illustrated by Tai Snaith. The images are created by hand using watercolour, gouache, pencil, pen and ink.

Tai would like to thank Luna Soo, Kate Tucker, Vexta and Paulina de Laveaux for all their generous support, encouragement, words of wisdom and keen eyes throughout the process of making this book. And thanks to Knotty for everything.

First published in Australia in 2012
by Thames & Hudson Australia Pty Ltd
11 Central Boulevard Portside Business Park
Port Melbourne Victoria 3207
ABN: 72 004 751 964

www.thameshudson.com.au

© Tai Snaith 2012
Reprinted 2014, 2015, 2018

ISBN: 978 050050 033 0

National Library of Australia
Cataloguing-in-Publication entry

Snaith, Tai.
The family hour : in Australia / Tai Snaith.
9780500500330 (hbk.)
Animals--Australia.

Editing: Nan McNab
Design: Lanz+Martin
Printed and bound in China by 1010 Printing

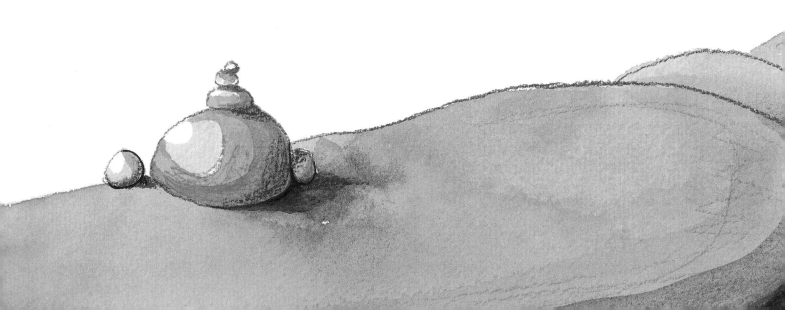